TEX-
MEX

KÖNEMANN

Talking Tex-Mex

The phrase 'Tex-Mex' isn't a trendy term coined by some food writer, or a funny name for a Mexican restaurant—it is a geographical fact. The border between Mexico and Texas may separate two very different countries, but where food is concerned, the line blurs.

Tex-Mex food relies heavily on traditional Mexican, and therefore often Spanish, ingredients and recipes, but there is also a strong American influence. While the origins are ancient, it is very modern food, quick and easy to prepare and, if you go easy on the cheese and sour cream, quite healthy. It is also great for vegetarians, with plenty of bean dishes. We are all familiar with Tex-Mex dishes such as tacos, nachos and chili con carne, whereas dishes such as tamales and chicken mole are less familiar, as are some of the ingredients. A glossary over the page explains the less well-known ingredients, while on this page are definitions of some Tex-Mex dishes (with the pronunciations where necessary), which will have you speaking fluent Tex-Mex in no time at all.

Burrito
(*ber-ee-toh*) Meaning literally 'little donkey', a burrito is a flour tortilla rolled around a savory filling of shredded beef, chicken or refried beans.

Chili Con Carne
A subject close to the heart of any Texan is chili. There are as many recipes for chili as there are cooks in Texas, each one touted as the best, the most authentic and the most traditional. Ironically, probably the least authentic version is the one most people are familiar with, based on ground beef, with tomatoes and kidney beans. A true Texan would deride it as a glorified Bolognese sauce, but of course we have included it in this book—for the gringos!

Chile Con Queso
(*chih-lee kon kay-soh*) Literally 'chile with cheese' (or cheese with chiles!)

Chimichanga
(chee-mee-chan-gah)
A flour tortilla filled usually with meat or chicken, folded envelope style and fried in oil until crisp.

Enchilada
(en-chuh-lah-da)
A corn tortilla filled with beans, beef or chicken, rolled, topped with tomato sauce and then baked.

Fajitas
(fah-hee-tuhs) Originally referring to the cut of meat (skirt steak), now understood as marinated beef, chicken or seafood, cooked on a sizzling cast-iron plate and served with salsa, cheese, guacamole and lettuce, with flour tortillas for wrapping.

Guacamole
Mashed avocado, often flavored with onion, cilantro, tomato and lime juice. Great as a dip or to accompany other Tex-Mex dishes.

Huevos Rancheros
(way-vohs rahn-cheh-ros) Huevos are eggs, rancheros means ranch-style. The eggs are poached or fried and served on crisp fried corn tortillas, with a tomato 'ranch' sauce. A great breakfast for curing a hangover!

Quesadilla
(keh-sah-dee-yah)
In Mexico, this is a turnover made from a corn pastry, filled and deep-fried. A Tex-Mex quesadilla, however, is two flour tortillas sandwiched together with cheese and beef, chicken, beans (or any leftovers that seem suitable!), and pan-fried. The simplest quesadilla, filled with cheese and chiles, is really a Tex-Mex grilled cheese sandwich.

Refried beans
This sounds like the beans have been fried twice, but it actually translates as 'well-fried' beans, meaning that after being boiled until tender, they are then fried until very soft.

Salsa Literally meaning just a 'sauce', salsa is, however, usually used to describe an uncooked condiment, such as tomato, onion and cilantro.

Tamales A dough is made from masa harina (see glossary), then wrapped in corn husks with a chicken or meat mixture, and steamed.

Tostadas A corn tortilla, fried to crisp, and topped with layers of beans, beef or chicken, cheese and salad.

3

ANCHO

BLACK BEANS

JALAPEÑOS

MASA HARINA

MULATO

Tex-Mex Glossary

If you can't get hold of some of the special chiles shown here, just use the more common long chiles or small hot red chiles instead.

Ancho

This deep-red dried poblano chile is the most common Mexican dried chile variety. It has a sweet, fruity flavor and a mild heat. The Ancho, along with the mulato and pasilla chiles, is considered one of the 'holy trinity' of chiles. Combined together, these 3 chiles are the essential ingredient in Mexican moles.

Black beans

Native to Yucatan, Mexico, these beans have purpley-black skins, creamy white flesh and a slightly smoky flavor. Black beans are also known as turtle beans and are available dried or canned. Do not confuse these beans with Asian fermented black beans.

Chili powder

Dried red chiles are finely ground to make this powder. The powders are marked 'hot' or 'mild', but the heat will differ between manufacturers. A Mexican chili powder is also often available.

Chayote

This pale, green, pear-shaped fruit is related to the gourd and was a staple food of the Aztecs and Mayas. It has a crisp texture and a subtle flavor suitable for braises and salsas.

Cilantro

Also known as Chinese parsley or fresh coriander, cilantro is an essential ingredient in salsas and sauces. The leaves have a fresh, pungent, peppery flavor and a bright green color, which complement spicy foods very well.

Cornmeal

Cornmeal is produced by grinding dried corn kernels. It is used as a thickener, filling or to coat, and is available in fine, medium or coarse grinds.

Habanero

Said to be the hottest of the fresh chiles, the habanero changes from green to orange to red, and can be used at any of these stages. It is one for the chili fanatic.

Jalapeño

This popular fresh chile is smooth and thick-fleshed and available in red or green. The skin sometimes has fine brown cracks running along it. Canned jalapeños are also often available.

Masa harina

Dried corn kernels are soaked, then finely ground to produce this flour, which can be white or blue and is used to prepare tamales, corn tortillas and corn chips.

Mulato

This dark brown chile is a variety of dried poblano. It has dried-fruit and chocolate flavors with moderate heat. It is one of the 'holy trinity' of chiles.

Pasilla

Also known as chile negro due to its blackish color, this dried chile is a member of the 'holy trinity' of chiles. Its deep, intense flavor ranges from raisin and berry to coffee and smoke.

Pepitas

Pepitas are green pumpkin seeds, which can be eaten lightly toasted as a snack or used to thicken and flavor moles and other sauces.

Pinto beans

A variety of red kidney beans, pintos have streaky reddish-brown skin, which becomes pink when cooked. Pintos can be replaced with red kidney beans if they are unavailable.

Poblano

This is a large, mild to hot chile with a thick flesh and subtle smoky flavor. It is usually roasted and stuffed, rather than chopped and added to dishes. When dried, it is called an Ancho chile.

Red kidney beans

Widely available in both dried and canned forms, these full-flavored beans have a dark red skin and creamy colored flesh.

Serrano

Available in red and green, this fresh chile is commonly used after it has matured to red. Smooth and moderately hot, it is often used in salsas and sauces.

Tomatillo

The shape and flavor of this green fruit resembles a small unripe tomato, but it is actually a member of the Cape gooseberry family. Tomatillos are available fresh or canned from speciality food stores.

PASILLA

PEPITAS

PINTO BEANS

POBLANO

TOMATILLOS

Tex-Mex

Most Tex-Mex dishes are quick and easy to make and taste delicious—great for a quick dinner or instead of fast food.

Beef Fajitas

Preparation time:
  30 minutes
  + overnight standing
Total cooking time:
  15 minutes
Serves 4

2 lb round steak, cut
  into thin strips
3/4 cup olive oil
2 tablespoons lime juice
4 cloves garlic, chopped
3 red chiles, chopped
2 tablespoons tequila
  (optional)
1 red sweet bell pepper,
  thinly sliced
1 yellow sweet bell
  pepper, thinly sliced
1 red onion, thinly
  sliced
8 flour tortillas (ready-
  made or see page 22)

1. Place the meat in a dish. Pour over the combined oil, lime juice, garlic, chiles and tequila and season with pepper. Cover and marinate overnight, turning once. Drain.

2. Preheat the oven to 300°F. Heat a cast-iron or heavy-based skillet. Add the meat in batches and cook over high heat for 4–5 minutes each side. Cool, then slice and toss with the peppers and onion.

3. Heat some oil in the pan over high heat. Place some of the meat mixture into the pan and toss well for about 2–3 minutes, searing the meat. Meanwhile, wrap the tortillas in foil and place in the oven for 10 minutes to soften. Place the fajitas on a serving plate and serve with the tortillas, shredded lettuce, Guacamole (see page 60), Fresh Corn and Tomato Salsa (see page 39) and sour cream.

NUTRITION PER SERVE
*Protein 120 g; Fat 60 g;
Carbohydrate 25 g; Dietary
Fiber 3 g; Cholesterol
335 mg; 1160 calories*

Beef Fajitas

Classic Quesadillas

Preparation time:
  15 minutes
Total cooking time:
  10 minutes
Serves 2–4

4 flour tortillas (ready-
  made or see page 22)
2 cups shredded
  Cheddar
6 green onions, finely
  chopped
4 jalapeño chiles,
  seeded and finely
  sliced

1. Brush 1 side of each
tortilla with a little oil.
Heat a skillet, then add
a tortilla, oiled-side-
down. Sprinkle with
half the Cheddar, green
onions and chile.
2. Put another tortilla
on top, oiled-side-up.
When the bottom is
lightly browned, place
a plate over the pan,
turn the quesadilla out,
then slide it back into
the pan, cooked tortilla
on top. Cook until the
quesadilla is brown and
the cheese melted, then
remove from the pan
and keep warm. Repeat
with the rest of the
tortillas and filling.
3. Cut into wedges and
serve with Fresh
Tomato Salsa.

*Classic Quesadillas (top), Fresh Tomato Salsa, and
Vegetarian Quesadillas (bottom)*

NUTRITION PER SERVE (4)
*Protein 20 g; Fat 30 g;
Carbohydrate 20 g; Dietary
Fiber 2 g; Cholesterol
60 mg; 400 calories*

Vegetarian Quesadillas

Preparation time:
  15 minutes + 1 hour
  standing
Total cooking time:
  2 hours 10 minutes
Serves 2–4

1 cup dried black
  beans
1 lb sweet potato, cut
  into thick slices
1 large red onion, cut
  into 8 wedges
1 1/4 cups crumbled feta
  cheese
3/4 cup shredded
  Cheddar
4 flour tortillas (ready-
  made or see page 22)

1. Place the black
beans in a saucepan,
cover with water and
bring to a boil. Turn off
the heat and let stand,
covered, for 1 hour.
Drain, refill with water,
bring to a boil and
simmer for 1 hour, or
until tender. Drain
and cool.
2. Brush the sweet
potato and onion
lightly with olive oil.
Roast in a 425°F oven
for 1 hour, turning

once, until tender. Cool
and chop. Combine the
drained beans and
vegetables in a bowl
with the feta and
Cheddar. Use this
filling to prepare the
quesadillas as
instructed at left.

NUTRITION PER SERVE (4)
*Protein 30 g; Fat 25 g;
Carbohydrate 50 g; Dietary
Fiber 10 g; Cholesterol
50 mg; 515 calories*

Fresh Tomato Salsa

Preparation time:
  5 minutes
Total cooking time:
  None
Serves 2–4

4 ripe tomatoes, finely
  chopped
1 small red onion,
  finely chopped
1 jalapeño or red
  chile, seeded and
  chopped
1/4 cup chopped
  cilantro
1 tablespoon lime
  juice

1. Combine all the
ingredients in a bowl
and mix well.
Cover with plastic
wrap and refrigerate
until ready to use.

NUTRITION PER SERVE (4)
*Protein 2 g; Fat 0 g;
Carbohydrate 4 g; Dietary
Fiber 2 g; Cholesterol
0 mg; 30 calories*

Breakfast Burritos

Preparation time:
  20 minutes
Total cooking time:
  45 minutes
Serves 4

1 lb 10 oz potatoes
1/4 cup butter
1 tablespoon oil
*4 flour tortillas (ready-
  made or see page 22)*
*4 green onions, finely
  chopped*
*8 eggs, lightly
  beaten*
*1 cup shredded
  Cheddar*
*1 cup Red Chili Sauce
  (see page 38)*
*1 cup Green Chili
  Sauce (see page 38)*

1. Preheat the oven to 300°F. Peel the potatoes and chop into cubes. Cook in a large saucepan of boiling salted water for about 20 minutes, or until just tender (don't overcook or they will go mushy). Drain well.
2. Heat half the butter and the oil in a heavy-based skillet, add the potatoes and cook for about 10 minutes over medium heat, or until golden brown, turning occasionally. Meanwhile, wrap the flour tortillas in foil and place in the oven for 10 minutes to soften.
3. In a separate skillet, melt the remaining butter, add the green onions and cook for 1 minute, then add the beaten eggs and cook until set, stirring occasionally.
4. To serve, place a quarter of the potatoes and a quarter of the egg mixture into the center of each softened tortilla, sprinkle each with a quarter of the shredded Cheddar and roll up. Spoon the chili sauces over the top and serve.

NUTRITION PER SERVE
*Protein 30 g; Fat 50 g;
Carbohydrate 60 g; Dietary
Fiber 10 g; Cholesterol
430 mg; 770 calories*

Huevos Rancheros

Preparation time:
  25 minutes
Total cooking time:
  30 minutes
Serves 4

1 red jalapeño chile
*3 large tomatoes, finely
  chopped*
*1 small onion, finely
  chopped*
*1 clove garlic,
  crushed*
*1 tablespoon chopped
  cilantro*
1/4 cup oil
*8 corn tortillas (ready-
  made or see page 22)*
8 eggs

1. Roast the chile by holding with tongs in a gas flame, or by flattening out and cooking under a preheated broiler, until the skin is black and blistered. Place in a plastic bag to cool, then scrape away the skin. Discard the seeds and finely chop the chile.
2. To make the tomato sauce, combine the chopped tomatoes with the onion, garlic, cilantro and jalapeño chile in a small saucepan. Bring to a boil, then reduce the heat and simmer for 10 minutes, or until the mixture has thickened.
3. Heat the oil in a skillet and cook the corn tortillas one at a time until warmed through and just crispy. Drain on paper towels and keep warm.
4. Fry the eggs a few at a time in the oil remaining in the skillet. To serve, arrange 2 tortillas on each plate. Top with the tomato sauce and 2 eggs. Serve immediately, with a spoonful of Refried Beans (see page 63) on the side.

NUTRITION PER SERVE
*Protein 20 g; Fat 25 g;
Carbohydrate 40 g; Dietary
Fiber 4 g; Cholesterol
360 mg; 450 calories*

Breakfast Burritos (top) with Huevos Rancheros

Red-Hot Ribs

Preparation time:
  10 minutes
  + marinating
Total cooking time:
  1 hour 20 minutes
Serves 4

3 lb pork spareribs
1 small onion, coarsely
  chopped
2 cloves garlic, chopped
2 small chiles, seeded
  and finely chopped
2 cups ketchup
1/4 cup firmly packed
  brown sugar
1 1/2 cups dark beer

1. Cut the spareribs
into pieces, with 3 or
4 ribs in each piece.
2. Put the onion, garlic
and chiles in a food
processor, and process
until finely chopped.
Add the ketchup, sugar
and beer and process
until combined.
3. Place the sauce
mixture into a large
pot. Add the ribs and
bring to a boil. Reduce
the heat and simmer
for 1 hour, partially
covered, moving the
ribs occasionally to
make sure they
cook evenly.
4. Taste the sauce and
add more chile if
desired. Transfer the
spareribs and the
marinade to a shallow,
nonreactive dish,
cover and refrigerate
for several hours
or overnight.
5. Drain the spareribs,
reserving the marinade,
and place on a greased
preheated barbecue
grill. Cook for about
15 minutes over high
heat, turning and
brushing occasionally
with the marinade. If
you like, heat the
remaining marinade
in a saucepan until
boiling and simmer for
5 minutes. Serve with
the ribs.

NUTRITION PER SERVE
*Protein 55 g; Fat 100 g;
Carbohydrate 35 g; Dietary
Fiber 2 g; Cholesterol
375 mg; 1394 calories*

Potato Skins with Chile Con Queso

Preparation time:
  20 minutes
Total cooking time:
  1 hour 20 minutes
Serves 4 as an appetizer

4 large potatoes
oil, for deep-frying

Chile Con Queso
2 tablespoons butter
2 green onions, finely
  sliced
1 small red chile, finely
  chopped
1 clove garlic, crushed
3/4 cup sour cream
2 cups shredded
  Cheddar

1. Preheat the oven
to 425°F. Bake the
potatoes for 1 hour,
turning once, or
until tender.
2. Let the potatoes cool
slightly, then cut in half
and scoop out the
insides, leaving about
1/2 inch of potato
inside the skin. Let the
skins cool completely,
then cut each one in
half again.
3. To make the chile
con queso, melt the
butter in a saucepan,
add the green onions,
chile and garlic and stir
over low heat for
1–2 minutes, or until
soft. Remove from the
heat and add the sour
cream and shredded
Cheddar. Return to the
heat and stir until the
mixture is smooth.
4. Half fill a large
saucepan with the oil
and deep-fry the potato
skins in batches until
they are crisp and
golden. Drain on paper
towels. Fill the skins
with the chile con
queso and serve with
Fresh Tomato Salsa
(page 9) and
Guacamole (page 60).

NUTRITION PER SERVE
*Protein 25 g; Fat 50 g;
Carbohydrate 35 g; Dietary
Fiber 4 g; Cholesterol
140 mg; 650 calories*

*Red-Hot Ribs (top) and
Potato Skins with Chile Con Queso*

Chicken Tamales

Preparation time:
45 minutes
Total cooking time:
1 hour 20 minutes
Serves 4

Dough
*1/2 cup butter,
softened*
*1 clove garlic,
crushed*
*1 teaspoon ground
cumin*
1 teaspoon salt
1 1/2 cups masa harina
*1/3 cup whipping
cream*
*1/3 cup chicken
stock*

*36 corn husks or pieces
of parchment paper*

Filling
1 cob sweet corn
2 tablespoons oil
*5 oz skinless, boned
chicken breast halves*
*2 cloves garlic,
crushed*

*1 red chile, seeded and
chopped*
1 red onion, chopped
*1 red sweet bell pepper,
chopped*
*2 tomatoes, peeled and
chopped*
1 teaspoon salt

1. To make the dough, use an electric mixer to beat the butter until creamy. Add the garlic, cumin and salt and mix well. Then alternately add the masa harina and combined cream and stock, and beat until smooth.
2. To make the filling, cook the corn in a saucepan of boiling water for 5–8 minutes, or until tender. Cool, then cut off the kernels. Heat the oil in a skillet and cook the chicken until golden. Remove, cool and shred the flesh with a fork. Add the garlic, chile and onion to the skillet and cook

until soft. Add the red pepper and corn and stir for 3 minutes. Add the chicken, tomatoes and salt and simmer for 15 minutes, or until the liquid has reduced.
3. Place the corn husks in a heatproof bowl. Cover with boiling water for 30 seconds, remove and drain. Spread a layer of dough over 12 of the husks, leaving a border at each end, then place each husk inside another. Place some filling on top and roll up. Place another husk on top to encase if necessary and secure the ends with string. Place in a steamer to cook for 35–40 minutes. Serve with Fresh Tomato Salsa (page 9).

NUTRITION PER SERVE
*Protein 15 g; Fat 40 g;
Carbohydrate 50 g; Dietary
Fiber 5 g; Cholesterol
110 mg; 640 calories*

Chicken Tamales

Remove the kernels from the corn cob by slicing downwards with a sharp knife.

Cover the corn husks with boiling water for 30 seconds to soften.

Spread a layer of the dough over 12 of the corn husks.

Place the chicken filling over the dough and roll up the husks.

Texan Beef Chile

Preparation time:
15 minutes
Total cooking time:
2 hours 15 minutes
Serves 4–6

4 lb chuck steak
flour, to coat
1/4 cup oil
2 onions, chopped
4 cloves garlic,
  crushed
2 tablespoons ground
  cumin
1 tablespoon chili
  powder
3 cups beef stock

1. Trim the meat of fat and sinew, and cut into small cubes. Toss in the flour until coated, then shake off the excess.
2. Heat the oil in a Dutch oven. Cook the meat in batches over moderate heat until browned, then remove from the pot. Add the onions and cook, stirring occasionally, until they are soft and golden.
3. Add the garlic, cumin and chili powder and cook, stirring constantly, for 1 minute. Return the meat to the pot and add the beef stock, stirring to scrape up the spices and juices from the bottom of the pot.

4. Bring to a boil, reduce the heat to very low and cook, covered, for 1¹/2 hours, or until the meat is tender. Stir occasionally, scraping the bottom of the pot to prevent the mixture from sticking. Remove the lid and cook for 30 minutes, or until the sauce is thick. Serve with rice.

NUTRITION PER SERVE (6)
Protein 70 g; Fat 20 g; Carbohydrate 5 g; Dietary Fiber 1 g; Cholesterol 220 mg; 470 calories

Empanadas

Preparation time:
30 minutes + cooling
Total cooking time:
1 hour
Makes 24

1 tablespoon oil
1 small onion, finely
  chopped
1 small green sweet bell
  pepper, finely chopped
1 clove garlic,
  crushed
3/4 lb lean ground beef
6 oz lean ground pork
1/2 cup tomato purée
2 tablespoons tomato
  paste
1/2 cup chopped green
  olives
1/4 cup dry sherry
*prepared pastry for two
  double-crust pies*
oil, for frying

1. Heat the oil in a skillet and cook the onion for 3 minutes, or until soft. Add the green pepper, cook for 3 minutes, then add the garlic and cook for 1 minute. Add the meat and cook, breaking up any lumps with a fork, until browned.
2. Stir in the tomato purée, tomato paste, chopped olives and sherry and bring to a boil. Reduce the heat and simmer for 10 minutes, stirring occasionally, or until most of the liquid has evaporated from the mixture. Season to taste and let cool.
3. Roll out the pastry thinly and cut into twenty-four 5 inch rounds. Place a heaped tablespoon of the filling onto each pastry round and fold over to encase the filling. Press the edges down with a fork to seal.
4. Heat 3/4 inch of the oil in a deep skillet to moderately hot. Cook the empanadas in batches until they are crisp and golden brown, then drain well on paper towels. Alternatively, bake in a 400°F oven for about 20–25 minutes.

NUTRITION PER EMPANADA
Protein 10 g; Fat 25 g; Carbohydrate 20 g; Dietary Fiber 1 g; Cholesterol 60 mg; 225 calories

Texan Beef Chilli (top) with Empanadas

Cilantro Tuna with Mango Salsa

Preparation time:
  25 minutes
  + marinating
Total cooking time:
  15 minutes
Serves 4

1 cup cilantro leaves
2 small red chiles,
  seeded and chopped
4 cloves garlic,
  chopped
1 1/4 inch piece fresh
  ginger, finely chopped
2–3 tablespoons olive
  oil
4 tuna steaks, about
  6 oz each

Mango Salsa
1 mango
1 small red onion,
  finely sliced
1/2 cup cilantro, finely
  chopped
2–3 tablespoons lime
  juice

1. Place the cilantro, chiles, garlic, ginger and oil in a food processor or pestle and mortar and process until it forms a paste. Spread in a thin coating over both sides of the tuna and marinate, covered, in the refrigerator for 1–2 hours.
2. To make the mango salsa, peel the mango and cut the flesh into small cubes. Combine with the onion, chopped cilantro and lime juice to taste. Marinate, covered, for 20 minutes.
3. Brush a barbecue grill or broiler rack with a little oil and heat until it starts to smoke. Cook the tuna for about 3–4 minutes each side for a medium-rare pink center. If you prefer your tuna well done, cook for another 2–3 minutes each side. Serve with the salsa.

NUTRITION PER SERVE
Protein 12 g; Fat 11 g; Carbohydrate 7 g; Dietary Fiber 2 g; Cholesterol 40 mg; 180 calories

Crab Cakes with Chili Mayonnaise

Preparation time:
  30 minutes + 1 hour
  refrigeration
Total cooking time:
  15 minutes
Serves 4

14 oz fresh crabmeat
1 cup fresh bread
  crumbs
2 green onions, finely
  chopped
1/2 cup cilantro leaves,
  finely chopped
2 eggs, lightly
  beaten
1/2 cup cornmeal
oil, for pan-frying

Chili Mayonnaise
1 egg yolk
1/2 teaspoon Dijon
  mustard
1 teaspoon white wine
  vinegar
1/2 cup chili oil

1. Mix the crab with the bread crumbs, green onions, cilantro and egg. Shape into 8 flat cakes.
2. Spread the cornmeal on a plate and coat each cake. Shake off any excess, place on a plate in a single layer, cover and chill for 1 hour.
3. To make the chili mayonnaise, combine the egg yolk, mustard and vinegar and beat for 1 minute, or until light and creamy. Add the oil slowly, whisking constantly. Season, cover and refrigerate.
4. Heat 1/4 inch of oil in a skillet. Cook the cakes in batches for 3–4 minutes on each side, or until golden. Drain on paper towels and serve with the chili mayonnaise.

NUTRITION PER SERVE
Protein 20 g; Fat 35 g; Carbohydrate 30 g; Dietary Fiber 1 g; Cholesterol 225 mg; 30 calories

Note: If fresh crab isn't available, use five 6 oz cans, drained.

Cilantro Tuna with Mango Salsa (top) and Crab Cakes with Chili Mayonnaise

Baked Snapper Yucatecan

Preparation time:
  10 minutes
Total cooking time:
  35 minutes
Serves 4–6

2 small red snapper or
  bream (porgy), about
  2 lb total, cleaned and
  scaled
2–3 tablespoons lime
  juice
1 tablespoon butter
1 tablespoon olive oil
1 small red sweet bell
  pepper, chopped
1 small green sweet bell
  pepper, chopped
1/2 red onion, finely
  chopped
1 teaspoon cumin seeds
1 teaspoon grated
  orange rind
1 tablespoon chopped
  cilantro leaves
1/3 cup pepitas
  (pumpkin seeds),
  toasted and chopped
1/3 cup orange juice
1 lime, cut into wedges,
  to garnish

1. Preheat the oven to
350°F. Loosely cover
the base of a large
roasting pan with a
piece of aluminum
foil and lightly grease
the center.
2. Rub the fish inside
and out with the lime
juice and season with
salt and black pepper.
Place in the center of
the foil, then pull the
sides up to form a
bowl shape.
3. Heat the butter and
olive oil in a skillet and
add the red and green
peppers, onion, cumin
seeds and orange rind
and cook over medium
heat, stirring, for about
2 minutes. Stir in the
cilantro and pepitas
and season to taste.
Spread this mixture
over the fish and pour
the orange juice over
the top. Loosely cover
with foil, folding the
sides of the 2 sheets
together to seal.
4. Bake for 30 minutes,
or until the flesh of the
fish flakes easily when
tested with a fork at the
thickest part. Remove
the foil and transfer to
a serving platter. Spoon
the juices over the fish
to moisten. Garnish
with the lime wedges.

NUTRITION PER SERVE (6)
*Protein 40 g; Fat 20 g;
Carbohydrate 5 g; Dietary
Fiber 2 g; Cholesterol
130 mg; 330 calories*

Note: For a special
occasion, you can wrap
the fish in banana
leaves instead of foil
to give a lovely flavor.
Banana leaves can be
found in Latin markets.

Corn and Sweet Potato Pudding

Preparation time:
  20 minutes
Total cooking time:
  1 hour
Serves 4–6

2 tablespoons olive
  oil
1 onion, grated
12 oz can creamed
  corn
1/2 cup cooked and
  mashed sweet potato
1/2 cup milk
1/2 cup whipping
  cream
3 eggs, lightly
  beaten
1 teaspoon salt

1. Preheat the oven to
350°F. Heat the oil in a
skillet. Fry the onion
until soft and place in a
large bowl.
2. Stir in the corn,
sweet potato, milk,
cream, eggs and salt
until combined.
3. Pour the mixture
into a lightly greased
4-cup baking dish and
bake for 45 minutes–
1 hour, or until the
pudding is puffed and
golden. Serve with a
salad and bread or as
an accompaniment to
meat dishes.

NUTRITION PER SERVE (6)
*Protein 6 g; Fat 14 g;
Carbohydrate 16 g; Dietary
Fiber 3 g; Cholesterol
120 mg; 210 calories*

*Baked Snapper Yucatecan (top) with
Corn and Sweet Potato Pudding*

FLOUR TORTILLAS

CORN TORTILLAS

Tex-Mex Breads and Chips

A Tex-Mex meal usually includes tortillas or breads. You can buy them ready-made for a quick meal, or make your own for a special occasion. Guacamole is the perfect accompaniment for corn chips.

Flour Tortillas

Sift 3 cups all-purpose flour and 1 teaspoon salt into a large bowl and make a well in the center. Using a flat-bladed knife, mix in 1/3 cup oil and up to 1 cup warm water until a soft dough forms. Place on an unfloured board and knead for 5 minutes, or until the dough is smooth and elastic. Put in a clean bowl, cover and place in a warm place for 1 hour. Divide the dough into 12 pieces, roll into balls and flatten and place on a lightly floured work surface. Roll each ball into an 8 inch circle and place in a stack covered by a layer of plastic wrap. Heat a heavy-based or cast-iron skillet over medium heat. Place a tortilla in the pan and cook for 1 minute. If the tortilla puffs up, gently push it down. Turn the tortilla over, cook for 1 minute, then serve. To store, cool the tortillas, then stack them on top of each other. The tortillas can be wrapped in foil when cold, then frozen. Reheat in the oven, microwave or a skillet. Makes 12 tortillas.

NUTRITION PER TORTILLA
Protein 3 g; Fat 7 g; Carbohydrate 23 g; Dietary Fiber 1 g; Cholesterol 0 mg; 165 calories

Corn Tortillas

Place 3 cups masa harina in a large bowl. Add 1 3/4 cups warm water. Using your hands, mix until the dough comes together to form a ball. Divide the dough into 12 even pieces and roll into balls. Flatten and place each ball between 2 layers of plastic wrap. Roll out to 7 inch rounds, trimming the edges to make neat circles. Cover, as the mixture dries out very easily. Heat a heavy-based or cast-iron skillet over medium heat. Place a tortilla in the pan and cook for 1 minute. Turn over

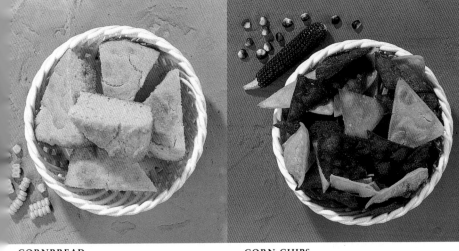

CORNBREAD **CORN CHIPS**

and cook for 1 minute. Turn again to the first side and cook for another 30 seconds, or until the tortilla puffs slightly but is still pliable. Remove and repeat with the remaining tortillas. Makes 12 tortillas.

NUTRITION PER TORTILLA
Protein 3 g; Fat 0 g; Carbohydrate 26 g; Dietary Fiber 1 g; Cholesterol 0 mg; 125 calories

Variation: To make blue corn tortillas, use blue masa harina.

Cornbread

Preheat the oven to 425°F. Generously brush an 8 inch cast-iron skillet (with an ovenproof or screw-off handle) or cake pan with corn oil. Place in the oven to heat while making the cornbread batter. Combine 1 cup cornmeal, 1 cup self-rising flour and 1 teaspoon salt in a large bowl and make a well in the center. Whisk together 1 egg, 1 cup buttermilk and 1/4 cup oil, pour into the dry ingredients and stir until the mixture is just combined, taking care not to overbeat. Pour into the pan, and bake for 25 minutes, or until the cornbread is light brown and firm. Cut into 8 wedges to serve.

NUTRITION PER WEDGE
Protein 4 g; Fat 9 g; Carbohydrate 30 g; Dietary Fiber 1 g; Cholesterol 25 mg; 220 calories

Corn Chips

Prepare 1 quantity of blue or white corn tortillas up to the stage just before cooking. Cut each tortilla into 8 wedges, split in half and allow to dry for 1 hour. Use enough corn or vegetable oil to half-fill a large deep saucepan or deep-fat fryer and heat to 375°F. Working in batches, fry the corn chips, stirring once or twice, for 1 minute, or until they are crisp but not brown. Remove with a slotted spoon, drain on paper towels and sprinkle with salt. The corn chips can be stored in an airtight container for a day. To reheat, put inside a paper bag and place in a 325°F oven for 10 minutes. Serves 4–6.

NUTRITION PER SERVE (6)
Protein 3 g; Fat 13 g; Carbohydrate 25 g; Dietary Fiber 1 g; Cholesterol 0 mg; 235 calories

Note: Serve 1 quantity of blue and 1 quantity of white corn chips together in a bowl for a great effect.

23

Beef Picadillo

Preparation time:
  10 minutes
Total cooking time:
  1 hour
Serves 4–6

1 onion, finely
  chopped
2 cloves garlic,
  crushed
1 1/2 lb lean ground beef
1/4 cup dry sherry
1/4 cup lime juice
2 tomatoes, peeled,
  seeded and chopped
1 tablespoon tomato
  paste
3 green serrano chiles,
  seeded and chopped
1/2 cup stuffed green
  olives, sliced
2 tablespoons capers
2 tablespoons golden
  raisins
1/2 cup beef stock
1 potato, cut into cubes
1 chayote or zucchini,
  cut into cubes
1 teaspoon ground
  cumin

1. Heat some oil in a
skillet and stir the
onion for 5 minutes, or
until golden. Add the
garlic, stir for 1 minute,
then add the beef.
Increase the heat and
cook, stirring
occasionally, for
10 minutes. Reduce the
heat, add the sherry
and lime juice and cook
for 5 minutes, then add
the tomatoes, tomato
paste, 2 chiles, olives,
capers, raisins and
stock. Cover and
simmer for 20 minutes.
2. Heat some oil in a
separate skillet, add the
potato, chayote or
zucchini and cumin.
Stir until brown, then
cook gently for
10 minutes. Add to the
beef mixture and cook
for 5 minutes. Top with
the remaining chile and
serve with Flour
Tortillas (page 22).

NUTRITION PER SERVE (6)
*Protein 30 g; Fat 15 g;
Carbohydrate 7 g; Dietary
Fiber 3 g; Cholesterol
80 mg; 300 calories*

Corn Dogs with Jalapeño Salsa

Preparation time:
  30 minutes +
  10 minutes standing
Total cooking time:
  35 minutes
Serves 8

3/4 cup coarse cornmeal
2 tablespoons sugar
1 egg
1/2 cup milk
1/4 cup butter, melted
1 cup all-purpose flour
1 1/2 teaspoons baking
  powder
oil, for deep-frying
flour, for coating
16 frankfurters
16 wooden skewers

Salsa
3–4 jalapeño chiles,
  seeded and chopped
2 cloves garlic, crushed
2/3 cup chopped green
  onion
8 large tomatoes, diced
2 tablespoons lime juice
2 tablespoons chopped
  cilantro

1. Combine the
cornmeal, 1 teaspoon
salt, sugar and 3/4 cup
boiling water. Cover
and let stand for
10 minutes. Stir the
egg, milk and butter
into the cormeal, then
sift in the flour and
baking powder and stir.
2. To make the salsa,
heat some oil in a
saucepan and fry the
chiles, garlic and green
onion for 1 minute.
Add the tomatoes,
cover and simmer for
20 minutes. Add the
lime juice and cilantro.
3. Heat the oil to 375°F.
Place the flour on
waxed paper. Insert a
skewer into each
frankfurter and coat in
the flour, then dip into
the cornmeal mixture.
Lower into the oil, 3 at
a time, turning until
golden. Drain, then serve
with the warm salsa.

NUTRITION PER SERVE
*Protein 20 g; Fat 40 g;
Carbohydrate 30 g; Dietary
Fiber 6 g; Cholesterol
100 mg; 550 calories*

*Beef Picadillo (top) and
Corn Dogs with Jalapeño Salsa*

Texan Chili Burgers

Preparation time:
25 minutes
Total cooking time:
40 minutes
Serves 4

Burgers
1 tablespoon ground cumin
1 teaspoon ground coriander
2 lb lean ground beef
1 onion, finely chopped
1 cup fresh bread crumbs
1 egg, lightly beaten
2 chiles, seeded and chopped
2 cloves garlic, crushed

Sweet Onion Relish
1 tablespoon oil
2 large onions, thinly sliced
1/4 cup firmly packed brown sugar
1 tablespoon cider vinegar

4 hamburger buns or bread rolls

1. To make the burgers, put the cumin and coriander into a dry skillet and stir over low heat for about 1 minute, or until fragrant. Combine with all the remaining burger ingredients in a bowl, using your hands to mix thoroughly. Divide the mixture into quarters and shape into patties 3/4 inch thick.
2. To make the relish, heat the oil in a saucepan, add the onions and cook over moderate heat, stirring occasionally, for 10 minutes, or until golden brown and soft. Stir in the brown sugar and vinegar and cook for 10 minutes more, stirring occasionally. Season to taste.
3. Brush a barbecue grill or skillet lightly with oil and heat to moderately hot. Cook the burgers for about 8 minutes on each side, turning only once during cooking. Split the hamburger buns and toast the insides. Serve the burgers on the buns or bread rolls, with some lettuce leaves, tomato slices, the sweet onion relish and a spoonful of sour cream.

NUTRITION PER SERVE
Protein 60 g; Fat 35 g; Carbohydrate 55 g; Dietary Fiber 5 g; Cholesterol 200 mg; 785 calories

Note: This recipe makes very large burgers. Divide the mixture into 6 portions for medium burgers.

Tex-Mex Roast Chicken

Preparation time:
20 minutes
Total cooking time:
50 minutes
Serves 4

2 x 2 lb chickens, washed and dried
1/4 cup olive oil
4 cloves garlic, crushed
4 teaspoons ground cumin
4 teaspoons ground coriander
4 teaspoons New Mexico chili powder or mild chili powder
1 teaspoon ground cinnamon
4 teaspoons flour

1. Preheat the oven to 400°F. Cut the chickens in half with poultry shears or a knife. Combine the oil and garlic and brush both inside and outside.
2. Combine the spices and flour in a bowl. Coat the chicken lightly and place on a rack in a roasting pan. Drizzle with a little oil and bake for about 45–50 minutes. Stand for 5 minutes, then serve with lime wedges.

NUTRITION PER SERVE
Protein 110 g; Fat 25 g; Carbohydrate 2 g; Dietary Fiber 0 g; Cholesterol 250 mg; 700 calories

Texan Chili Burgers (top) with Tex-Mex Roast Chicken

Chicken Tacos

Preparation time:
  20 minutes
Total cooking time:
  15 minutes
Serves 4

1 onion, finely chopped
2 cloves garlic,
  crushed
3 tomatoes, chopped
1 chile, seeded and
  chopped
1 teaspoon sugar
1 barbecued chicken
8 large taco shells
4 lettuce leaves, shredded
1 1/2 cups shredded
  Cheddar

1. Preheat the oven to 350°F. Heat some oil and cook the onion for 3 minutes. Add the garlic and cook for 1 minute. Add the tomatoes, chile and sugar, bring to a boil, reduce the heat and simmer for 5 minutes, or until thick. Season.
2. Remove the flesh from the chicken and shred, using 2 forks to pull apart. Stir into the sauce. Heat the taco shells in the oven for 5 minutes.
3. To serve, fill the tacos with the chicken, lettuce and cheese.

NUTRITION PER SERVE
*Protein 14 g; Fat 22 g;
Carbohydrate 6 g; Dietary
Fiber 3 g; Cholesterol
50 mg; 330 calories*

Seafood Burritos

Preparation time:
  45 minutes
Total cooking time:
  40 minutes
Serves 4

1/3 cup oil
1/3 cup butter
2 cloves garlic,
  crushed
3 small red chiles,
  seeded and chopped
8 oz plain cleaned sea
  scallops, thawed
1 lb medium raw
  shrimp, shelled and
  deveined
1 lb salmon fillet, cut
  into small pieces
4 flour tortillas (ready-
  made or see page 22)
3 tablespoons all-
  purpose flour
1/2 cup whipping
  cream
3/4 cup milk
1/2 cup sour cream
1/3 cup grated
  Parmesan
2 tablespoons chopped
  fresh parsley
1 cup shredded
  Cheddar

1. Preheat the oven to 325°F. Heat the oil and half of the butter in a skillet. Add the garlic and chiles and cook for 1 minute. Add the scallops and cook for 2–3 minutes, then remove and drain on paper towels. Add the shrimp and cook for 2–3 minutes; drain on paper towels. Add the salmon, cook for 3–4 minutes, then remove and drain on paper towels. Place all of the seafood in a large bowl.
2. Wrap the tortillas in aluminum foil and place in the oven for 10 minutes to warm. In a saucepan, melt the remaining butter, add the flour and stir until the mixture begins to bubble. Remove from the heat and gradually stir in the cream and milk. Return to the heat and whisk until the sauce thickens and boils. Stir in the sour cream, grated Parmesan and parsley, pour over the seafood and mix well.
3. Fill each warmed tortilla with the seafood mixture and roll up. Place in a lightly greased baking dish, sprinkle with the shredded cheese and bake for about 15–20 minutes, or until heated through and the cheese has melted. Serve on hot Red Chili Sauce (page 38).

NUTRITION PER SERVE
*Protein 80 g; Fat 90 g;
Carbohydrate 30 g; Dietary
Fiber 2 g; Cholesterol
440 mg; 1215 calories*

Chicken Tacos (top) with Seafood Burritos

Remove the seeds from the chiles, using rubber gloves to protect your hands.

Add the steak to the onion and spices and turn with tongs to coat well.

Beef Chimichangas

Preparation time:
  30 minutes
Total cooking time:
  2 hours 50 minutes
Serves 4

2 tablespoons oil
1 large onion, finely
  chopped
1 clove garlic, crushed
2 teaspoons ground
  cumin
½ teaspoon ground
  cinnamon
2 chiles, seeded and
  chopped
2 lb round steak
2 cups beef stock
4 flour tortillas
  (ready-made or see
  page 22)
oil, for frying

1. Heat the oil in a large saucepan and cook the onion over medium heat for 10 minutes, or until very soft and golden brown. Add the garlic, cumin, cinnamon and chiles and cook, stirring, for another minute.

2. Add the steak and stir to coat with the spices, then stir in the stock, scraping the bottom of the pan. Bring just to a boil, reduce the heat and gently simmer, covered, for 1 hour. Uncover and cook for another 1–1½ hours, or until the liquid has just about evaporated. Stir frequently towards the end of the cooking time to prevent burning on the bottom of the pan.

3. Shred the meat, using 2 forks to pull it apart, then let it cool.

4. Preheat the oven to 325°F. Wrap the tortillas in foil and place in the oven for 10 minutes to soften. Remove from the oven and leave wrapped for another 5 minutes. Working with one at a time (and leaving the other tortillas wrapped as you work), place a quarter of the meat on one tortilla, and fold in the sides to encase. Set aside, fold-side-down, while you fill the remaining tortillas.

5. Heat about 3/4 inch of oil in a skillet to moderately hot. Place a few chimichangas fold-side-down in the pan for 2–3 minutes, then turn and cook the other side for 2–3 minutes, or until golden and crisp. Repeat with the rest of the chimichangas. Drain on paper towels. Serve immediately with some Red Chili Sauce (page 38) and Mexican Rice (page 63).

NUTRITION PER SERVE
Protein 60 g; Fat 20 g; Carbohydrate 20 g; Dietary Fiber 2 g; Cholesterol 170 mg; 535 calories

Beef Chimichangas

Shred the beef, using 2 forks to pull the meat apart.

Place a quarter of the meat onto each tortilla and fold in the sides to encase.

Bean Tostadas

Preparation time:
  30 minutes
Total cooking time:
  15 minutes
Serves 4

2 tomatoes, chopped
1 small red onion,
  finely chopped
1 small red chile, finely
  chopped
1/4 cup finely chopped
  cilantro
2 tablespoons oil
4 corn tortillas (ready-
  made or see page 22)
16 oz Refried Beans
  (ready-made or see
  page 63)
4 lettuce leaves,
  shredded
1 cup shredded
  Cheddar
1 avocado, sliced
1/3 cup sour cream
sliced black olives, to
  garnish

1. Combine the
tomatoes, onion, chile
and cilantro in a bowl,
cover and set aside.
Heat the oil in a heavy-
based skillet and cook
the tortillas, one at a
time, for 1–2 minutes
on each side, or until
they are crisp. Drain
on paper towels. Warm
the refried beans in
a skillet.
2. To assemble, spread
each tortilla with the
refried beans, then top
with the lettuce, tomato
mixture and Cheddar.
Arrange the avocado,
sour cream and olives
on top.

NUTRITION PER SERVE
*Protein 10 g; Fat 50 g;
Carbohydrate 15 g; Dietary
Fiber 10 g; Cholesterol
30 mg; 540 calories*

Chicken Enchiladas

Preparation time:
  40 minutes
Total cooking time:
  1 hour 10 minutes
Serves 4

2 large red chiles
2 large green chiles
1 tablespoon oil
1 onion, finely
  chopped
2 cloves garlic,
  crushed
1 cup chicken stock
1 cup tomato purée
1 barbecued chicken
8 corn tortillas
  (ready-made or
  see page 22)
1 cup shredded
  Cheddar

1. Roast the chiles by
holding with tongs one
at a time in a gas flame,
or flatten out and cook
under a hot broiler,
until the skins are black
and blistered. Cool in a
plastic bag, then peel,
discard the seeds and
chop finely.

2. Heat the oil in a
saucepan and add the
onion. Cook over low
heat for 5 minutes, or
until the onion is soft.
Add the garlic and
cook for 1 more
minute. Add the chiles,
stock and tomato
purée, bring to a boil,
reduce the heat and
simmer for 15 minutes.
Season the sauce with
salt and pepper.
3. Preheat the oven to
350°F. Remove the
flesh from the chicken
and shred finely, using
2 forks to pull the meat
apart. Heat a little oil
in a heavy-based skillet
and cook the tortillas,
one at a time, for about
1 minute each side, or
until soft and warm but
not crisp. Drain on
paper towels.
4. Spread 1/4 cup of the
tomato sauce into the
bottom of a large
baking dish. Fill the
tortillas with the
chicken and roll up.
Arrange in the dish,
pour the remaining
sauce over the top and
and sprinkle with the
Cheddar. Bake for
20 minutes, or until the
enchiladas are cooked
through and the cheese
has melted.

NUTRITION PER SERVE
*Protein 40 g; Fat 40 g;
Carbohydrate 8 g; Dietary
Fiber 3 g; Cholesterol
165 mg; 535 calories*

Bean Tostadas (top) with Chicken Enchiladas

Chili Con Carne

Preparation time:
  20 minutes
Total cooking time:
  1 hour 20 minutes
Serves 4–6

1 tablespoon oil
1 large onion,
  chopped
2 cloves garlic,
  crushed
1 teaspoon chili
  powder
4 teaspoons ground
  cumin
2 lb lean ground beef
16 oz can crushed
  tomatoes
1 cup beef stock
1 teaspoon dried
  oregano
2 teaspoons sugar
2 tablespoons tomato
  paste
12 oz can red kidney
  beans, rinsed and
  drained

1. Heat the oil in a
large saucepan and add
the onion. Cook over
medium heat for
5 minutes, or until the
onion is soft and
golden. Add the garlic,
chili and cumin, and
cook for 1 minute.
2. Add the meat and
cook for 5 minutes, or
until browned, breaking
up any lumps with a
fork as it cooks.

3. Stir in the tomatoes,
stock, oregano and
sugar. Bring to a boil,
reduce the heat and
simmer, partially
covered, for 1 hour,
stirring occasionally.
4. Stir in the tomato
paste and beans and
season to taste. Cook
for 5 minutes to heat
the beans, then serve
with cornbread to mop
up the juices.

NUTRITION PER SERVE (6)
*Protein 40 g; Fat 20 g;
Carbohydrate 15 g; Dietary
Fiber 6 g; Cholesterol
100 mg; 405 calories*

Cornbread with Chiles and Cheese

Preparation time:
  30 minutes
Total cooking time:
  1 hour
Serves 4–6

1 small red sweet bell
  pepper
2 long red chiles
2 long green chiles
1/2 cup shredded
  Cheddar
2 cups fine cornmeal
1/3 cup sugar
2 teaspoons baking
  powder
1 teaspoon baking
  soda
13 oz can creamed corn

1/2 cup buttermilk or
  soured milk
1 cup shredded
  Cheddar, extra

1. Preheat the oven to
375°F. Grease a round
7-cup baking dish.
2. Cut the sweet pepper
into quarters and
remove the seeds and
membrane. Place the
pepper and chiles under
a preheated broiler and
cook until the skins
blister and blacken.
Remove from the
broiler, place in a
plastic bag to cool, then
peel. Remove the seeds
and membrane from
the chiles and cut the
sweet pepper and chiles
into fine strips.
3. Combine the
shredded Cheddar,
cornmeal, sugar, baking
powder and baking
soda in a large bowl
and mix well. Add the
creamed corn,
buttermilk and the chile
and pepper strips and
mix gently until
combined. Spoon the
mixture into the baking
dish and smooth the
top with the back of
the spoon. Sprinkle
with the extra shredded
Cheddar and bake for
40 minutes, or until the
cornbread has risen and
is set in the center.

NUTRITION PER SERVE (6)
*Protein 10 g; Fat 12 g;
Carbohydrate 70 g; Dietary
Fiber 3 g; Cholesterol
35 mg; 425 calories*

*Chili Con Carne (top) and
Cornbread with Chiles and Cheese*

Chicken Mole

Preparation time:
  1 hour + 35 minutes
  soaking
Total cooking time:
  2 hours
Serves 4–6

3 lb 4 oz *chicken*
6 *cloves garlic*
2 *onions, chopped*
1³/4 oz *mulato*
  chiles
2 oz *pasilla chiles*
2 oz *ancho chiles*
3 *whole cloves*
3 *whole allspice*
2 *teaspoons dried*
  thyme
2 *teaspoons dried*
  marjoram
2 *teaspoons dried*
  oregano
¹/4 *cup sesame*
  seeds
¹/4 *cup unsalted*
  peanuts
8 *almonds*
2 *tablespoons raisins*
3 *cinnamon sticks,*
  slivered
3 oz *Mexican drinking*
  chocolate or
  bittersweet chocolate

1. Preheat the oven to
375°F. Cut the chicken
into 8 pieces, wash and
rinse well. Place in a
saucepan with 4 cloves
garlic and half the
onions. Pour in enough
water to cover
completely, bring to a
boil, then reduce the
heat to a simmer and
cook for 30 minutes, or
until just tender.
Remove the chicken
and strain the stock,
reserving just over
4 cups.
2. Cut the chiles open
and remove and reserve
the seeds. Bake the
chiles for 5 minutes,
then place them in a
bowl, cover with water
and soak them for
30 minutes.
3. Place the chile seeds
in a dry skillet. Cook
over medium heat,
shaking to brown
evenly. Once the seeds
have browned, increase
the heat and char until
black. Place in a bowl,
cover with water and
soak for 5 minutes.
Drain the seeds and
place in a blender or
food processor with
²/3 cup water, the
cloves, allspice, thyme,
marjoram and oregano.
4. Heat 1 tablespoon of
oil in a heavy-based
skillet. Add the sesame
seeds and fry until dark
brown. Add to the
blender or food
processor, leaving any
extra oil in the pan.
Blend well.
5. Heat another
tablespoon of oil. Add
the peanuts, almonds
and raisins and cook
until the nuts are
golden and the raisins
puff up, stirring
constantly. Place in the
blender. Add the
remaining onion and
garlic and the
cinnamon to the skillet,
cook until golden, then
add to the blender.
Blend until the mixture
becomes a thick paste,
adding a little water if
necessary. Heat some
oil in a large saucepan,
add the chili paste and
fry for 15 minutes,
scraping the pan
occasionally to prevent
it from sticking.
6. Place half the chiles
in the clean blender
with ¹/2 cup of the chili
soaking liquid and
blend until smooth,
adding more liquid if
the mixture becomes
too thick. Add the
remaining chiles and
more liquid and blend
until the mixture is
smooth. Add to the pan
with the chocolate, mix
well and simmer for
5 minutes. Add 4 cups
of the stock and stir
until the mixture is well
combined. Bring to a
boil and simmer for
35 minutes. Add the
chicken pieces, season
with salt to taste and
cook for about
10 minutes. Add a little
more stock to thin the
sauce if necessary.

NUTRITION PER SERVE (6)
Protein 75 g; Fat 50 g;
Carbohydrate 20 g; Dietary
Fiber 4 g; Cholesterol
225 mg; 820 calories

Chicken Mole

FRESH CORN
AND TOMATO
SALSA

MIXED SWEET
PEPPER SALSA

PEACH AND
GINGER SALSA

Sauces and Salsas

A Tex-Mex sauce is cooked, while a salsa is a mixture of raw ingredients. Just a spoonful of sauce or salsa on the side will add extra zing to your Tex-Mex meal.

Red Chili Sauce

Roast 2 large fresh red chiles by placing them under a preheated broiler or holding with tongs in an open gas flame, until the skin is black and blistered. Cool in a plastic bag, then peel the skin and remove the seeds and stems. Dry-fry 1 teaspoon ground cumin in a saucepan for 30 seconds, or until fragrant. Combine the chiles, cumin, a 12 oz can tomatoes, 1 small chopped red onion, 1 crushed clove garlic, $1/2$ cup chicken stock and 2 teaspoons red wine vinegar in a food processor and blend until smooth. Transfer to a saucepan, bring to a boil, then reduce the heat and simmer for 20 minutes. Refrigerate the sauce, covered, for up to 2 days. Serve warm or at room temperature. Makes $1^{1}/2$ cups.

NUTRITION PER SERVE
Protein 1 g; Fat 0 g; Carbohydrate 4 g; Dietary Fiber 1.4 g; Cholesterol 0 mg; 20 calories

Green Chili Sauce

Combine 2 large fresh green chiles, a 10 oz can drained tomatillos, 1 small onion, 1 crushed clove garlic and $1/2$ cup chicken stock in a food processor and blend until smooth. Transfer to a saucepan and bring to a boil. Reduce the heat to medium and simmer for 10 minutes. Refrigerate, covered, for up to 2 days. Serve warm or at room temperature. Makes 1 cup.

NUTRITION PER SERVE
Protein 2 g; Fat 0 g; Carbohydrate 5 g; Dietary Fiber 2 g; Cholesterol 0 mg; 30 calories

Mixed Sweet Pepper Salsa

Finely chop 1 small red, 1 small yellow and 1 small green sweet bell pepper and place in a large mixing bowl. Add 1 finely chopped red onion, 5 finely sliced green onions and $1/4$ cup finely chopped cilantro. Stir in 2–3 tablespoons of lime juice, according to taste. Mix together gently until the salsa is well combined and serve immediately. Serves 4.

NUTRITION PER SERVE
Protein 1 g; Fat 0 g; Carbohydrate 3 g; Dietary Fiber 1 g; Cholesterol 0 mg; 20 calories

Fresh Corn and Tomato Salsa

Bring a large saucepan of salted water to a boil and cook 2 cobs of sweet corn in the boiling water until tender. Cool completely, then remove the kernels by cutting downwards with a sharp knife. Place in a large mixing bowl. Seed and finely chop 1 ripe tomato and add to the corn kernels along with 1 seeded and finely chopped green jalepeño chile, 1 finely chopped red onion, 1/4 cup chopped cilantro and 2–3 tablespoons lime juice, according to taste. Mix until all of the ingredients are well combined and serve the salsa immediately. Serves 4.

NUTRITION PER SERVE
Protein 1 g; Fat 0 g; Carbohydrate 7 g; Dietary Fiber 1 g; Cholesterol 0 mg; 40 calories

Melon and Chili Salsa

Place 2 cups finely diced honeydew melon into a bowl. Add 1 finely chopped red onion, 2 seeded and finely chopped small red chiles and 1/4 cup finely chopped cilantro. Mix until well combined. Stir in 2–3 tablespoons freshly squeezed lime juice, according to taste. Serve the salsa immediately. Serves 4.

NUTRITION PER SERVE
Protein 0 g; Fat 0 g; Carbohydrate 2 g; Dietary Fiber 0 g; Cholesterol 0 mg; 15 calories

Peach and Ginger Salsa

Peel and finely dice 3 ripe peaches. Place in a large bowl with 2 teaspoons finely grated fresh ginger, 2 tablespoons finely sliced green onions, 1/4 cup chopped cilantro and 2–3 tablespoons lime juice, according to taste. Mix until all of the ingredients are well combined and serve the salsa immediately. Serves 4.

NUTRITION PER SERVE
Protein 0 g; Fat 0 g; Carbohydrate 2 g; Dietary Fiber 0 g; Cholesterol 0 mg; 8 calories

MELON AND CHILI SALSA

RED CHILI SAUCE

GREEN CHILI SAUCE

Chicken Tostadas

Preparation time:
  45 minutes
Total cooking time:
  30 minutes
Serves 4

8 corn tortillas (ready-
  made or see page 22)
oil, for deep-frying
1 lb skinless, boned
  chicken breast halves
1 teaspoon black
  pepper
1/2 teaspoon paprika
4 large lettuce leaves,
  shredded
1 1/4 cups shredded
  Cheddar
2 avocados, sliced
1/3 cup sour cream
4 green onions, sliced
  on the diagonal

1. Preheat the oven to
325°F. Wrap the
tortillas in foil and
place in the oven for
10 minutes to warm.
Heat the oil in a deep
saucepan. Using
2 gaufrette baskets, one
smaller than the other,
place 1 tortilla in the
larger basket and place
the smaller basket on
top. Keep the other
tortillas covered. Deep-
fry until crisp and
golden, then drain on
paper towels. Repeat
with the remaining
tortillas.
2. Sprinkle the chicken

with the pepper and
paprika. Heat some oil
in a skillet and cook
for 4–5 minutes each
side. Cool slightly, then
slice thinly.
3. Fill the tortilla
baskets with the
lettuce, shredded
Cheddar, chicken slices,
avocado, a spoonful of
sour cream, the green
onions and some Fresh
Tomato Salsa (see
page 9).

NUTRITION PER SERVE
*Protein 40 g; Fat 50 g;
Carbohydrate 4 g; Dietary
Fiber 3 g; Cholesterol
130 mg; 650 calories*

Seafood Fajitas

Preparation time:
  30 minutes
Total cooking time:
  20 minutes
Serves 2

3 ripe tomatoes, finely
  chopped
1 small red chile, finely
  chopped
2 green onions, finely
  sliced
10 oz medium raw
  shrimp, peeled,
  deveined and halved
8 oz plain cleaned sea
  scallops, thawed and
  halved
8 oz boneless white fish
  fillets, cut into bite-
  size cubes
1/3 cup lime juice

1 clove garlic, crushed
1 avocado
2 tablespoons lemon
  juice
4 flour tortillas (ready-
  made or see page 22)
1 onion, sliced
1 green sweet bell
  pepper, cut into thin
  strips

1. Preheat the oven to
325°F. Combine the
tomatoes, chile and
green onions in a bowl,
then season to taste.
2. Combine the shrimp,
scallops, fish, lime
juice and garlic in a
nonreactive dish. Cover
and set aside.
3. Slice the avocado
and brush with the
lemon juice to prevent
browning. Wrap the
tortillas in foil and
place in the oven for
10 minutes to soften.
4. Heat a lightly oiled
chargrill or cast-iron
skillet to very hot, add
the onion and green
pepper and cook,
turning occasionally,
until soft and light
brown; push to one
side. Drain the seafood
and cook briefly until
it is seared and just
turns opaque.
5. To serve, wrap the
seafood mixture,
tomato mixture and
avocado in the tortillas.

NUTRITION PER SERVE
*Protein 85 g; Fat 45 g;
Carbohydrate 50 g; Dietary
Fiber 9 g; Cholesterol
350 mg; 960 calories*

Chicken Tostadas (top) with Seafood Fajitas

Cheese and Bean Nachos

Preparation time:
30 minutes
Total cooking time:
15 minutes
Serves 4

3 tomatoes, finely
  chopped
1 small red onion,
  finely chopped
1/4 cup chopped
  cilantro
1 small red chile, finely
  chopped
2 x 12 oz cans red
  kidney beans, rinsed
  and drained
2 x 7 oz packages corn
  chips
2 cups shredded
  Cheddar
1 large avocado
1/3 cup sour cream
2 green onions, finely
  sliced

1. Preheat the oven to
350°F. Combine the
tomatoes, onion,
cilantro and chile in a
bowl. Place the kidney
beans in a saucepan,
cover with water and
bring to a boil. Drain
and return to the pan.
Add 1/2 cup of the
tomato mixture and
cook for 5 minutes,
stirring often.
2. Place the bean
mixture in a shallow
baking dish and cover
with the corn chips.
Sprinkle with the

shredded Cheddar and
bake for 3–5 minutes,
or until the cheese
melts. Transfer to
serving plates.
3. Spread the remaining
tomato mixture over
the melted cheese, then
lightly mash the
avocado and place it on
top, with a spoonful of
sour cream and the
sliced green onions.

NUTRITION PER SERVE
*Protein 40 g; Fat 80 g;
Carbohydrate 90 g; Dietary
Fiber 30 g; Cholesterol
95 mg; 1230 calories*

Beef with Black Bean Salsa

Preparation time:
  30 minutes + 1 hour
  30 minutes standing
Total cooking time:
  1 hour 30 minutes
Serves 4–6

1/2 cup dried black
  beans
1 small red sweet bell
  pepper
1 small onion, finely
  chopped
3 cloves garlic, crushed
1 cob sweet corn,
  kernels removed
2 tomatoes, chopped
1/2 cup chopped
  cilantro
1/4 cup lime juice
4 tenderloin steaks
  (filet mignon)

1. Place the beans in a
saucepan and cover
with water. Bring to a
boil, then remove from
the heat, cover and let
stand for 1 hour. Drain
and rinse well. Return
to the pan, cover with
water, bring to a boil
and simmer for 1 hour,
or until tender. Drain.
2. Cut the red pepper in
quarters and remove
the seeds and membrane.
Place under a preheated
broiler and cook until
the skin blisters and
blackens. Cool in a
plastic bag, then peel
and cut into strips.
3. Heat some oil in a
skillet, cook the onion
until soft, add the garlic
and corn and cook for
4 minutes. Place in a
bowl with the red
pepper, beans,
tomatoes, cilantro and
lime juice. Marinate,
covered, for 30 minutes.
4. Lightly oil a chargrill
pan or cast-iron skillet
and heat until it begins
to smoke. Brush the
steaks with oil and
cook for 3–4 minutes
on each side for
medium, or a little
longer for well-done.
Let stand for 5 minutes,
then serve with salsa.

NUTRITION PER SERVE (6)
*Protein 20 g; Fat 3 g;
Carbohydrate 10 g; Dietary
Fiber 4 g; Cholesterol
45 mg; 150 calories*

---

*Cheese and Bean Nachos (top) and
Beef with Black Bean Salsa*

Place the chiles under a preheated broiler to blacken and blister their skins.

Place the chiles in a plastic bag to cool, then peel away the skin.

Chiles Rellenos (Stuffed Chiles)

Preparation time:
  30 minutes
Total cooking time:
  20 minutes
Serves 4 as an appetizer

8 green poblano
  chiles
1 cup shredded
  Cheddar
flour, for dusting
3 eggs, separated
oil, for frying
1 cup Red Chili Sauce
  (see page 38)

1. Roast the chiles by placing under a preheated broiler or holding carefully, one at a time, with tongs in an open gas flame, until the skin is black and blistered. Cool in a plastic bag, then carefully peel away the skin. Cut a slit in each chile lengthwise and remove the seeds and membrane, taking care not to break the chile flesh.

2. Stuff the chiles with the cheese and press the slit closed, or secure with a cocktail pick. Dust with the flour and shake off the excess.

3. Whisk the egg whites until foamy, then add some salt and beat until stiff peaks form. Beat in the yolks, one at a time, until just combined.

4. Heat the oil about 3/4 inch deep in a skillet. Dip the chiles into the egg, then fry, in batches, for 4–5 minutes, or until golden. Drain on paper towels and remove the cocktail picks. Serve on a bed of red chili sauce.

NUTRITION PER SERVE
Protein 20 g; Fat 15 g; Carbohydrate 15 g; Dietary Fiber 10 g; Cholesterol 165 mg; 295 calories

Chiles Rellenos

Slit the chiles lengthwise, then remove the seeds and membrane.

Dust the stuffed chiles with the flour, then dip into the egg mixture.

Spicy Cowboy Beans

Preparation time:
  20 minutes + 1 hour standing
Total cooking time:
  1 hour 40 minutes
Serves 4–6

2 1/2 cups dried red
  kidney beans
2 tablespoons oil
4 slices bacon,
  chopped
1 large onion,
  chopped
2 teaspoons chili
  powder
2 tablespoons
  Worcestershire sauce
1/4 cup firmly packed
  brown sugar
4 cups vegetable or beef
  stock

1. Place the beans in a large saucepan and cover with water. Bring to a boil, remove from the heat and let stand, covered, for 1 hour. Drain well.
2. Heat the oil in a large saucepan and add the chopped bacon and onion. Cook, stirring occasionally, until the onion is golden and the bacon brown. Add the chili powder and cook, stirring, for 30 seconds.
3. Add the beans, Worcestershire sauce, sugar and vegetable or beef stock. Bring to a boil, reduce the heat to very low and cook, covered, for 1 1/2 hours, stirring occasionally and scraping the bottom of the pan to prevent the mixture from sticking. Serve sprinkled with a little shredded Cheddar.

NUTRITION PER SERVE (6)
Protein 8 g; Fat 8 g; Carbohydrate 20 g; Dietary Fiber 4 g; Cholesterol 10 mg; 170 calories

Note: This dish tastes even better the next day. Thin with a little water if necessary when reheating.

Baked Honey and Garlic Ribs

Preparation time:
  20 minutes +
  overnight marinating
Total cooking time:
  55 minutes
Serves 4–6

2 1/2 lb pork spareribs
1/2 cup honey
6 cloves garlic,
  crushed
2 inch piece fresh
  ginger, finely grated
1/4 teaspoon Tabasco
3 tablespoons chili
  sauce
2 teaspoons grated
  orange rind

1. Cut the spareribs into small pieces, with about 2–3 bones per piece. Place in a large dish. Combine the remaining ingredients and pour over the ribs. Turn the ribs in the marinade until they are well coated. Leave in the refrigerator overnight to marinate if possible.
2. Preheat the oven to 400°F. Drain the ribs and place the marinade in a small saucepan. Place the ribs in 1 or 2 large shallow baking dishes in a single layer.
3. Bring the marinade to a boil and simmer gently for 3–4 minutes, or until it has thickened and reduced slightly.
4. Brush the spareribs with the marinade and place in the oven. Cook for 50 minutes, basting with the marinade 3–4 times. Cook until the ribs are a rich golden color and are well browned. Serve the spareribs with jacket-baked potatoes topped with a spoon of sour cream and a sprinkling of fresh chives.

NUTRITION PER SERVE (6)
Protein 35 g; Fat 70 g; Carbohydrate 25 g; Dietary Fiber 1 g; Cholesterol 250 mg; 930 calories

Spicy Cowboy Beans (top) and Baked Honey and Garlic Ribs

Black Bean and Roast Garlic Dip

Preparation time:
30 minutes + 1 hour standing
Total cooking time:
2 hours 10 minutes
Serves 4

1/2 cup dried black beans
1 head garlic, cloves peeled and separated
2 tablespoons chopped cilantro
1/3 cup lime juice
1/4 cup sour cream
pinch of chili powder
dash of Tabasco sauce

1. Place the black beans in a saucepan, cover with water and bring to a boil. Turn off the heat and let stand, covered, for 1 hour. Drain, refill with water, bring to a boil and simmer for 1 1/2 hours, until tender.
2. Meanwhile, preheat the oven to 350°F. Place the garlic on a baking sheet, drizzle with some oil and bake for 25–30 minutes, or until the garlic is soft.
3. Place the beans in a large bowl and mash with a fork until they begin to break down

and become slightly smooth. Mix in the crushed garlic, cilantro, lime juice, sour cream, chili powder and Tabasco sauce.
4. Serve the dip with some Corn Chips or with some Cornbread (see page 23) sliced into 1/2 inch thick triangles and fried in a little oil until golden brown.

NUTRITION PER SERVE
Protein 3 g; Fat 4 g; Carbohydrate 3 g; Dietary Fiber 2 g; Cholesterol 13 mg; 60 calories

Margarita Chicken with Black Bean Salsa

Preparation time:
20 minutes + 1 hour standing + 2–4 hours marinating
Total cooking time:
1 hour 15 minutes
Serves 6

6 skinless, boned chicken breast halves
1/3 cup tequila
1 cup lime juice
1 cup dried black beans
1/3 cup olive oil
1 teaspoon honey
1 clove garlic, crushed

16 oz can corn kernels, drained
1 red onion, finely chopped
1/2 cup cilantro leaves, chopped

1. Place the chicken in a nonreactive dish and pour in the combined tequila and 2/3 cup of the lime juice. Refrigerate, covered, for 2–4 hours, turning occasionally.
2. Place the beans in a saucepan, cover with water and bring to a boil. Turn off the heat and let stand, covered, for 1 hour. Drain, refill with water, bring to a boil and simmer for 1 hour, or until tender. Combine the remaining lime juice, oil, honey and garlic in a screw-top jar and shake until combined.
3. Drain the beans and allow to cool. Place the beans in a bowl with the corn, onion and cilantro. Pour the dressing over and toss to mix.
4. Heat a lightly oiled barbecue grill or chargrill pan. Remove the chicken from the marinade and cook for 4–5 minutes each side. Serve with the black bean salsa.

NUTRITION PER SERVE
Protein 45 g; Fat 15 g; Carbohydrate 25 g; Dietary Fiber 9 g; Cholesterol 80 mg; 450 calories

Black Bean and Roast Garlic Dip (top) and Margarita Chicken with Black Bean Salsa

Tex-Mex Fried Chicken

Preparation time:
  15 minutes + 2 hours marinating
Total cooking time:
  30 minutes
Serves 4

2 lb chicken pieces, washed and dried
2 cups buttermilk
oil, for deep-frying
1¹/2 cups all-purpose flour

1. Place the chicken in a bowl and pour in the buttermilk. Mix well. Cover and refrigerate for 2 hours, turning occasionally.
2. Half-fill a large, deep saucepan with oil and heat to 350°F. Place the flour in a shallow dish and season with salt and pepper. Remove a piece of chicken from the buttermilk, shake off any excess, dip into the flour and coat well. Lower the chicken into the oil, in batches, and deep-fry for 12 minutes on each side, making sure that the oil is not too hot. Drain the chicken well on paper towels.

NUTRITION PER SERVE
Protein 70 g; Fat 30 g; Carbohydrate 40 g; Dietary Fiber 2 g; Cholesterol 135 mg; 680 calories

Charred Shrimp with Red Pepper Mayonnaise

Preparation time:
  20 minutes + 2 hours marinating
Total cooking time:
  40 minutes
Serves 4

2 lb large raw shrimp
4 cloves garlic, crushed
¹/4 cup lime juice
1 teaspoon ground cumin
¹/2 cup cilantro leaves, chopped
lime wedges, to serve

Red Pepper Mayonnaise
1 small red sweet bell pepper
6 cloves garlic, unpeeled
1 tablespoon olive oil
¹/3 cup whole-egg mayonnaise
1 tablespoon lemon juice

1. Peel and devein the shrimp, leaving the tails intact. Combine the crushed garlic, lime juice, cumin and cilantro in a bowl, place the shrimp in the marinade and mix well. Cover and refrigerate for at least 2 hours.

2. To make the red pepper mayonnaise, preheat the oven to 375°F. Cut the red pepper into quarters and remove the seeds and membrane. Place on a baking sheet with the garlic and drizzle with the olive oil. Roast for 20–30 minutes, or until the skin blisters on the pepper and the garlic is soft but not burnt. Place in a plastic bag until cool, then peel the skin off the pepper and garlic.
3. Place in a food processor with the mayonnaise and process until fairly smooth. Place in a bowl and stir in the lemon juice.
4. Preheat a lightly oiled chargrill pan or cast-iron skillet until it just starts to smoke. Drain the shrimp, discarding the marinade, and cook for 2 minutes on each side, or until cooked. You may need to do this in batches, depending on the size of your pan. Serve the shrimp with the red pepper mayonnaise and a wedge of lime.

NUTRITION PER SERVE
Protein 50 g; Fat 15 g; Carbohydrate 8 g; Dietary Fiber 2 g; Cholesterol 380 mg; 370 calories

Tex-Mex Fried Chicken (top) and Charred Shrimp with Red Pepper Mayonnaise

Stuffed Sopaipillas

Preparation time:
20 minutes
+ 20 minutes resting
Total cooking time:
45 minutes
Serves 4

Sopaipillas
4 cups all-purpose flour
1¹/2 teaspoons baking powder
4 teaspoons butter
1¹/2 cups boiled milk, cooled
oil, for deep-frying
1 cup Red Chili Sauce (see page 38)
1¹/2 cups shredded Cheddar

Filling
2 tablespoons oil
1 lb lean ground pork
1 red onion, chopped
1/4 teaspoon cayenne pepper
1 clove garlic, crushed
1/2 cup chicken stock
6 oz Refried Beans (ready-made or see page 63)
2 tablespoons chopped cilantro

1. To make the sopaipillas, combine the all-purpose flour, baking powder and 1¹/2 teaspoons salt in a bowl. Rub in the butter and mix until it resembles bread crumbs. Gradually work in the milk until the dough is stiff and springy. Knead 15–20 times, or until the dough is smooth, then rest, covered, for 20 minutes.
2. To make the filling, heat the oil and add the pork, onion, cayenne pepper and garlic; season, then cook for 10 minutes. Add the stock, simmer for 10 minutes, then add the beans and cilantro.

3. Preheat the oven to 350°F. Divide the dough into 8 even pieces and place on an unfloured surface. Roll each piece into a 1/4 inch thick, 4 inch square. Keep covered.
4. In a saucepan, heat 2¹/2 inches of oil to about 350°F. Lightly stretch each square, then place in the oil. Hold under for 20 seconds each side, or until puffed and golden. Drain on paper towels.
5. Slit each sopaipilla open at one end and spoon in the filling. Place in a baking dish and spoon some of the chili sauce and shredded Cheddar over the top. Bake for 15 minutes, then serve with extra chili sauce.

NUTRITION PER SERVE
Protein 35 g; Fat 45 g; Carbohydrate 100 g; Dietary Fiber 9 g; Cholesterol 80 mg; 930 calories

Stuffed Sopaipillas

Pour in the milk and mix with a flat-bladed knife until the dough is stiff.

Knead the dough on a lightly floured surface until it is smooth.

With tongs, hold a square of the dough under the hot oil until puffed and golden.

Slit each sopaipilla at one end and spoon in the filling.

Spicy Mexican Meatball Soup

Preparation time:
  20 minutes
Total cooking time:
  30 minutes
Serves 4

8 oz lean ground
  beef
8 oz lean ground
  pork
3/4 cup cooked white
  rice
1 egg, lightly
  beaten
1/2 teaspoon chili
  powder
1/2 teaspoon paprika
1 teaspoon salt
2 tablespoons olive oil
1 small onion, diced
1 clove garlic,
  crushed
1 1/4 cups tomato purée
4 cups beef stock
1/4 cup finely chopped
  fresh oregano

1. Combine the beef, pork, rice, egg, chili powder, paprika and salt in a bowl. Shape into balls the size of walnuts and set aside.
2. Heat the oil in a saucepan and gently fry the onion and garlic over medium-low heat until soft. Stir in the tomato purée and beef stock. Bring to a boil and drop in the meatballs. Cover and simmer for about 20 minutes.
3. Serve sprinkled with some chopped oregano.

NUTRITION PER SERVE
Protein 20 g; Fat 30 g; Carbohydrate 12 g; Dietary Fiber 2 g; Cholesterol 90 mg; 430 calories

Corn and Cilantro Soup

Preparation time:
  20 minutes
Total cooking time:
  50 minutes
Serves 4–6

8 cobs sweet corn
1 large red sweet bell
  pepper
2 tablespoons oil
1 onion, finely
  chopped
2 cloves garlic,
  crushed
3 cups chicken stock
1/2 cup lime juice
1/3 cup cilantro leaves

1. Preheat a barbecue grill or broiler. Remove the husks and silk from the corn cobs and cook on the barbecue or broil for about 10 minutes, turning frequently, until roasted and slightly blackened. Cool, then cut the kernels from the cobs with a small, sharp knife. (Hold the cobs vertically on a chopping board and run the knife down the sides of the cobs.)
2. Cut the red pepper into quarters. Discard the seeds and membrane and cook under the broiler or on the barbecue until the skin has blackened and blistered. Remove from the heat and place in a plastic bag to cool. Peel away the skin and finely chop the flesh.
3. Heat the oil in a large saucepan, and cook the onion for 5 minutes, or until very soft and light golden. Add the garlic and cook for 1 minute.
4. Add the corn kernels, red pepper and chicken stock to the saucepan, bring to a boil, reduce the heat and simmer, partially covered, for about 20 minutes.
5. Cool the soup slightly, then purée half of it in a blender or food processor until the mixture is fairly smooth. Transfer all of the soup to a clean pan to heat through (do not boil). Just before serving, stir in the lime juice and the cilantro leaves.

NUTRITION PER SERVE (6)
Protein 8 g; Fat 9 g; Carbohydrate 50 g; Dietary Fiber 8 g; Cholesterol 0 mg; 310 calories

Spicy Mexican Meatball Soup (top) with Corn and Cilantro Soup

Fried Onion Rings

Preparation time:
  10 minutes
Total cooking time:
  20 minutes
Serves 4–6 as a snack

2 large onions
1 1/2 cups all-purpose
  flour
2 teaspoons ground
  cumin
1 teaspoon paprika
1 1/2 cups cold beer
oil, for deep-frying
Red Chili Sauce (see
  page 38) or sweet chili
  sauce, to serve

1. Cut the onions into
rings about 1/2 inch
wide. Sift the flour and
spices together into a
large bowl, make a well
in the center and slowly
pour in the beer. Stir in
lightly with a fork until
just combined, taking
care not to overbeat or
the batter will not be
light and crisp. The
mixture should be
slightly lumpy.
2. Half-fill a large
saucepan with the oil.
Heat until moderately
hot (when a bread cube
dropped in becomes
crisp and golden in
45 seconds, the oil is
ready). Dip the onion
rings into the batter,
allowing the excess to
drip off, then deep-fry
in batches until crisp
and golden. Drain well

on paper towels.
Season with salt, then
serve with the red chili
or sweet chili sauce on
the side.

NUTRITION PER SERVE (6)
*Protein 5 g; Fat 15 g;
Carbohydrate 40 g; Dietary
Fiber 0 g; Cholesterol
30 mg; 310 calories*

Chili Chicken Chimichangas

Preparation time:
  40 minutes
Total cooking time:
  30 minutes
Serves 6

4 skinless, boned
  chicken breast
  halves
2 teaspoons black
  pepper
1 teaspoon chili
  powder
1/2 cup oil
2 cloves garlic
1/2 teaspoon chili
  powder, extra
1 lb button
  mushrooms, sliced
6 flour tortillas (ready-
  made or see page 22)
Fresh Tomato Salsa (see
  page 9)

1. Preheat the oven to
325°F. Sprinkle the
chicken with the
pepper and chili
powder. Heat half the
oil in a skillet, add the

chicken and cook for
about 3–4 minutes on
each side, or until
cooked through. Cool,
then shred into fine
pieces, using 2 forks to
pull the meat apart.
Add the remaining oil
to the pan and lightly
fry the garlic and extra
chili powder for
1 minute. Add the
mushrooms and stir-fry
for about 3–4 minutes.
Add the chicken and
toss gently to combine.
Set aside.
2. Wrap the tortillas in
foil and place in the
oven for 10 minutes to
soften. Work quickly
with one tortilla at a
time, keeping the others
covered with the foil.
Place some filling in the
center and top with
2 tablespoons of the
tomato salsa. Fold in
the sides and roll up
like an envelope.
3. Heat a little oil in a
skillet. Place 1–2 filled
tortillas in the hot oil at
once, turning carefully
to cook both sides until
they are golden. Serve
with the remaining
tomato salsa, some
Mexican Rice (page 63)
and a spoonful of
sour cream.

NUTRITION PER SERVE
*Protein 6.5 g; Fat 30 g;
Carbohydrate 25 g; Dietary
Fiber 5 g; Cholesterol
50 mg; 340 calories*

*Fried Onion Rings (top) with
Chili Chicken Chimichangas*

Rub the butter into the flour mixture
until it resembles bread crumbs.

Pour in the beef stock and stir into the
mixture with a flat-bladed knife.

Tamale Beef and Bean Pie

Preparation time:
  40 minutes
Total cooking time:
  1 hour 30 minutes
Serves 6–8

1 tablespoon oil
1 large onion, finely
  chopped
1 lb lean ground
  beef
3 cloves garlic,
  crushed
1/2 teaspoon chili
  powder
16 oz can crushed
  tomatoes
1 cup beef stock
16 oz can red kidney
  beans, drained
2 1/2 cups masa
  harina
1 teaspoon baking
  powder
1/2 cup butter,
  cut into cubes and
  chilled
1 1/2 cups beef stock
2 cups shredded
  Cheddar

1. Heat the oil in a skillet. Add the onion and cook gently until soft and transparent. Increase the heat, add the beef and cook until brown. Add the garlic, chili, tomatoes and stock. Bring to a boil, then simmer for 30 minutes, or until the liquid has evaporated to a thick sauce. Stir in the beans and cool.
2. Lightly grease a deep 9 inch baking dish. Place the masa harina, baking powder and 1/2 teaspoon salt in a bowl. Rub in the butter until the mixture resembles bread crumbs. Using a knife, mix in the stock, then use your hands to bring the mixture together into a ball. Divide in half and roll one half between 2 sheets of parchment paper to fit the dish.
3. Push the pastry into the dish and up the side, not worrying if the pastry cracks. Trim the edge.
4. Preheat the oven to 400°F. Place the filling into the pastry-lined dish and sprinkle with half of the shredded Cheddar. Roll out the remaining pastry in the same way as before. Brush the edge with water and place on top of the pie. Trim the edge and press the 2 layers of pastry together to seal. Sprinkle with the remaining Cheddar and bake for 45 minutes, or until the pastry is crisp and slightly puffed. Decorate with a little sour cream to serve.

NUTRITION PER SERVE (8)
Protein 25 g; Fat 30 g; Carbohydrate 10 g; Dietary Fiber 5 g; Cholesterol 110 mg; 435 calories

Tamale Beef and Bean Pie

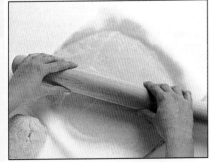

Divide the dough in half and roll out 1 half between sheets of parchment paper.

Spoon the beef and bean filling into the dish, then sprinkle with cheese.

Guacamole

Preparation time:
30 minutes
Total cooking time:
None
Serves 6 as a side dish

3 avocados
1 small tomato
1–2 red chiles, finely
  chopped
1 small red onion,
  finely chopped
1 tablespoon chopped
  cilantro
1 tablespoon lime juice
2 tablespoons sour
  cream
1–2 drops habanero or
  Tabasco sauce

1. Cut the avocados in
half, discarding the skin
and stone. Coarsely
chop, then mash lightly
with a fork.
2. Cut the tomato in
half horizontally. Using
a teaspoon, scoop out
the seeds and discard.
Finely dice the flesh and
add to the avocado.
3. Stir in the chiles,
onion, cilantro, lime
juice, sour cream and
habanero or Tabasco
sauce. Season with
cracked black pepper.
4. Serve immediately, or
cover wih plastic wrap
and refrigerate for up
to 2 hours, removing
30 minutes before
serving to allow the
guacamole to reach
room temperature.

NUTRITION PER SERVE
*Protein 1 g; Fat 8 g;
Carbohydrate 1 g; Dietary
Fiber 0 g; Cholesterol
2 mg; 70 calories*

Note: Habanero sauce
is a very hot sauce
made from habanero
chiles. Use sparingly to
add extra zing.

Beef Tacos

Preparation time:
30 minutes
Total cooking time:
20 minutes
Serves 4

1 tablespoon oil
1 onion, finely
  chopped
2 cloves garlic, finely
  chopped
1/4 teaspoon chili
  powder
1 teaspoon ground
  paprika
1 teaspoon ground
  cumin
1 teaspoon ground
  coriander
1/2 teaspoon dried
  oregano
1 teaspoon sugar
1 lb lean ground beef
2 tablespoons tomato
  paste
12 small taco shells
4 large lettuce leaves,
  shredded
1 1/2 cups shredded
  Cheddar
Fresh Tomato Salsa (see
  page 9), to serve

1. Preheat the oven to
350°F. Heat the oil in a
large skillet. Add the
chopped onion and
cook over low heat
until softened but not
browned. Add the
garlic and cook for
another minute. Stir in
the chili powder,
paprika, cumin,
coriander, oregano, the
sugar and a teaspoon
of salt. Cook over
medium heat for
3–4 minutes.
2. Increase the heat,
add the ground beef
and cook until the meat
is browned. Add the
tomato paste and about
1/4 cup water, making
sure that the pan is hot
so that most of the
water evaporates. Stir
the mixture constantly
for 5–10 minutes. If the
beef sticks, add a little
more water. The
mixture will be quite
dry looking, but will
have plenty of flavor.
3. Heat the taco
shells in the oven for
5 minutes. Place the
meat on the table with
the taco shells,
shredded lettuce,
shredded Cheddar and
tomato salsa and let
everyone assemble the
tacos themselves.

NUTRITION PER SERVE
*Protein 40 g; Fat 40 g;
Carbohydrate 4 g; Dietary
Fiber 2 g; Cholesterol
125 mg; 525 calories*

Guacamole (top) and Beef Tacos

Creamed Corn

Preparation time:
  15 minutes
Total cooking time:
  5 minutes
Serves 8 as a side dish

16 oz can corn
  kernels
4 teaspoons cornstarch

1. Drain the corn kernels, reserving the liquid. Add a little water to the liquid if necessary to make up ³/4 cup. Place half of the corn kernels in a food processor with the reserved liquid and process until smooth.
2. Transfer to a heavy-based saucepan. In a bowl, mix the cornstarch with a little water to form a smooth paste.
3. Add the cornstarch paste to the pan with the remaining corn kernels and stir over medium heat until the mixture thickens and boils. Set aside to cool slightly as the mixture will thicken on standing. Serve as a side dish.

NUTRITION PER SERVE
*Protein 0 g; Fat 0 g;
Carbohydrate 3 g; Dietary
Fiber 0 g; Cholesterol
0 mg; 16 calories*

Mexican Rice

Preparation time:
  10 minutes
Total cooking time:
  25 minutes
Serves 8 as a side dish

1 tablespoon olive
  oil
1 small onion,
  chopped
1 clove garlic,
  chopped
1 cup long-grain white
  rice
¹/2 cup tomato purée
1 cup chicken stock

1. Heat the oil in a large saucepan, add the onion and cook for 5 minutes, or until soft. Add the garlic and cook for 1 minute. Add the rice and stir for 1–2 minutes, or until well coated in the oil.
2. Add the tomato purée and stock to the pan and bring to a boil. Reduce the heat to very low, cover tightly with a lid and simmer for 25 minutes, or until the liquid is absorbed and the rice tender. Fluff up the grains with a fork, and serve as a side dish.

NUTRITION PER SERVE
*Protein 2 g; Fat 3 g;
Carbohydrate 20 g; Dietary
Fiber 1 g; Cholesterol
0 mg; 115 calories*

Refried Beans

Preparation time:
  10 minutes +
  overnight soaking
Total cooking time:
  1 hour 45 minutes
Serves 8 as a side dish

1 cup dried pinto, red
  kidney or black beans
1 small onion,
  halved
3 cloves garlic
¹/4 cup oil

1. Place the dried beans in a bowl, cover with water and soak overnight. Drain. Place in a heavy-based saucepan and cover with water.
2. Add the onion and garlic, bring to a boil, reduce the heat and simmer for 1¹/2 hours, or until tender. Cool, then remove the onion and garlic. Drain the beans, reserving ¹/2 cup of the liquid.
3. Heat the oil in a heavy-based skillet. Add half the beans and mash. Stir in half the liquid, then add the remaining beans and liquid and mash to a thick purée. Serve at once, or refrigerate for up to 2 days.

NUTRITION PER SERVE
*Protein 4 g; Fat 7 g;
Carbohydrate 4 g; Dietary
Fiber 3 g; Cholesterol
0 mg; 95 calories*

*Creamed Corn (top), Mexican Rice, and
Refried Beans (bottom)*

Index